Why Is My Hair Curly?

lakshmi iyer

illustrated by
niloufer wadia

RED PANDA

To Anjali, Meghna and Sahana for lighting up my world.
To Narayanan, for being the wind beneath my wings.
To Amma, for being my rock.
To Appa, for being my hero.

WHY IS MY HAIR CURLY?

Lakshmi Iyer is a banking professional in her day job. She slaves over her writing at night when her children are in bed.

An MBA graduate from LeBow College of Business and an alumna of the Yale Writer's Workshop, she writes creative non-fiction primarily, on her personal website www.lgiyer.com. She hopes to publish a memoir of her adoption journey some day.

When Lakshmi is not working or writing, she enjoys cooking and watching random food videos on YouTube. She lives with her husband and her three daughters (two adopted and one biological) near Philadelphia, in the US.

RED PANDA

First published by Red Panda, an imprint of Westland Publications
Private Limited, in 2020

1st Floor, A Block, East Wing, Plot No. 40, SP Infocity, Dr MGR Salai,
Perungudi, Kandanchavadi, Chennai 600096

Westland, the Westland logo, Red Panda and the Red Panda logo are the
trademarks of Westland Publications Private Limited, or its affiliates.

Copyright © Lakshmi Iyer, 2020

ISBN: 9789389648119

This is a work of fiction. Names, characters, organisations, places, events and
incidents are either products of the author's imagination or used fictitiously.

Contents

All Vacations Come to an End

'We both get window seats!' said Avnish, his face lit up with joy as he surveyed the seats of the Shatabdi coach they were in. While he stood figuring out which one he wanted, Avantika put her backpack down on the seat that had its back to the direction they were to travel in. She loved the feeling of being pulled backwards—of having no idea where she was going. Also, she hated the wind that got in her face and messed up her already unruly hair. Amma had tied a scarf around it for good measure.

35 Avnish M8
36 Avantika F10
37 Shanthi F68
40 Radha F38
41 Francis M38
42 Venkatraman M72

Avantika also loved looking at the passenger charts they stuck on the coach, before people boarded. She would look at the names of people, who would sit near them, and always wished there would be other children she could make friends with. This time too, they were out of luck. The others on the list seemed like an older couple who had requested aisle seats.

Amma and appa were busy putting away their suitcases and humongous boxes that paati and thatha, her grandparents, had packed for all of them. They were filled with vaadam, or sun-dried fryums; palapazham, also called jackfruit; maavadu, the baby mango pickle special to Coimbatore and loads of bakshanam, a mix of sweet and savoury snacks to share with friends once they reached home. It was not that they could not get what they wanted in Chennai, but paati always liked to make a fuss of her son and his family when they visited.

'Look! Chithappa and thatha are here!' Avantika pointed to her appa's younger brother and father. They were making their way through the aisle towards them.

'Here's something for you kutties.' Chithappa's eyes twinkled as he held out a bag each for them. They were crammed full of chocolate bars and cream biscuits—just the things they loved during a long train journey. Avantika flew into her chithappa's arms when he held them out. Avnish joined her, and they stayed like that for a bit before thatha reminded them that it was almost time for the train to leave.

'Avni, aren't you going to eat your chocolate?

I can eat it for you, if you like,' Avantika teased, knowing it would distract him from feeling sad when the train left. It worked, as Avnish unwrapped his chocolate bar and scarfed it down before Avantika could even unwrap hers!

The train started moving slowly, picking up speed as it pulled out of the station. Avantika peered out of the window until the station disappeared from view. The end of vacation was always sad.

It had been a fun few weeks, Avantika thought, as she pulled out her journal to write about her vacation. She had promised her teacher that she would keep a journal over the holidays.

She wrote 'Fabulous Four' at the top of the page, then scowled and erased it. It was a good thing she was writing with a pencil. It had been a good trip till the time their cousins Vishnu and Visruth had joined. They were a year older—fraternal twins who looked nothing like each other. They had a common interest, though:

5

teasing Avantika. Avnish seemed to fly under the radar, aligning himself with them when it suited him and joining Avantika when they were out of sight.

This time, they had taken to calling Avantika 'Medusa'. She had no idea who that was. She looked it up on her iPad and saw this woman with a head full of snakes. Was her hair really like that?! Or perhaps they meant her hair could hide a hundred snakes? Who knew what those boys thought!

Avantika was sensitive about her hair. She had thick curls that framed her face, and no amount of combing and brushing could keep them down. Living in Chennai meant her hair became frizzy and untamed. She spent a considerable amount of time standing in front of the mirror, quite frustrated to see those unruly locks heading out in every direction. Each strand seemed to have a mind of its own, starting a mutiny right on top of her head. No one in her home, not her amma, not her appa, not even Avnish, had hair like hers. It sometimes bothered her that she did not have the shiny, sleek hair the rest of her family had.

Then there was the thing about Avantika and Avnish being adopted.

For as long as she could remember, amma and appa had been open about their adoption. In fact, Avantika couldn't even remember the first time they spoke about it.

Each year, amma would make rava kesari, a dish both Avnish and she liked, on their homecoming day—the day they were legally adopted by amma and appa and became a part of their family. Amma (and sometimes appa) would talk to them about how three-and-a-half-year-old Avantika had been spunky and bright-eyed and Avnish had been such a sweet baby that both amma and appa had fallen in love with them at first sight.

All of them would finish the day looking at photographs from their parents' first visit to the orphanage to see them. There were pictures with that frail old paati who had taken care of them, and Kalpana akka and Sister D'Souza, who ran the orphanage. There were other children in the pictures that amma said were her friends, but Avantika did not remember their names now.

The four of them had gone back to the ashram before it closed down for good. Avantika and Avnish ran to the swings to play with the other children, while amma and appa went to Sister D'Souza's office. They emerged after almost an hour. When Avantika asked amma what had taken them so long, she just hugged her tight. Amma looked very sad when they left. The last picture they had taken there was a selfie of the four of them near the signboard.

Avantika was curious. She was sure amma would have told her about the conversation they had with Sister D'Souza had she asked. But because she thought it would upset amma, she never brought up that closed-door discussion ever again.

Nothing was ever brushed under the carpet in their family, least of all feelings. There were no secrets either. Avantika knew amma and appa loved her and Avnish, which is why her being adopted didn't bother her much. Well … most times.

Avantika usually thought of being adopted when she was particularly frustrated with her hair, which, frankly, was most days. On those days, she thought about who could have had hair like hers. Her birth mother? Her birth father? Someone in the family who had given her and Avnish up? She longed to know and to see features like hers on another person in her birth family.

She also thought about being adopted when some people, like her cousins, tossed it at them like it was an insult. It hurt her that her cousins felt that she and Avnish were inferior to them because of being adopted. If only they knew how much amma, appa, paati, thatha and chittappa loved her and Avnish. Harumph! She knew if she mentioned it to amma or appa, her cousins would be in trouble. But then, the thought of having to talk about it to chithi, their chithappa's wife, was enough to keep her quiet. Chithi had never liked them, Avantika was not sure why.

Was it because of her hair that stood out like the rakshashis in Amar Chithra Katha?

Or maybe because her skin was the colour of caramel, warm and brown?

Was it because her amma and appa were always carrying on about Avni this, Avanti that?

Or maybe because everyone knew that paati and thatha loved her best?

Who knew? In any case, she was not going to talk to anyone about it. She just had to bear them for the summer vacations, and then they would go home!

Paati was Avantika's favourite family member. She was a complete rockstar! Besides giving the warmest bear hugs, she also sneaked in some kaapi decoction into Avantika's milk when her mom was not looking. Paati knew that amma did not like to give them coffee. She saved the crispiest bits from the potato fries for her and Avnish. Most of all, she believed Avantika when she said that her chithi and cousins were mean to her. Paati would mutter under her breath and tell Avantika that they did not know how to appreciate good things and that Avantika and Avnish were the best things that had happened to their family. Well, the feelings were mutual … paati was the best thing to have happened to her after amma and appa.

So, yes, her vacation had been a mixed bag. Another week and they would be back in school. It was all too much to write, especially for something to share at school. She sighed loudly and closed her journal. She would write after she reached home.

'Amma, I am bored. Can I have some snacks?' Avantika asked, knowing how much it annoyed her amma. Avantika loved annoying amma. When amma was mad, she would crinkle her nose, her eyes would go wide, and Avantika could almost see that she was trying hard not to yell. All Avantika could do was stifle her giggles because that really would cause amma to yell.

She was such a hog that amma often referred to her stomach as a bottomless pit. So she had half-expected amma to scowl at her and ask her to go read or play. Instead, amma wordlessly handed over some murukku, the handmade deep-fried crunchy snack her paati made so well.

'Amma, can I have one more murukku?' Avnish asked, adding a please belatedly. 'Just one more …' He took a chance, but amma playfully swatted his hand away.

'If you eat any more, your tummy will burst!' she said and made a horrified face. All of them burst out laughing. Sighing, Avnish pulled out his Rubik's cube instead.

'Want to play I spy?' Avantika asked, truly bored out of her mind.

'I spy with my little eye … something purple!' Avnish shouted.

'The clothesline!' Avantika replied after scanning the countryside through the glass windows of the train. The purple skirt had caught her eye almost immediately.

'My turn. I spy with my eye …' Avantika looked for something unique and saw a factory belching smoke into the air.

' … something grey!'

Avnish looked around and called out, 'Clouds? Road? Dustbin?'

Avantika kept saying 'No!' with glee and watched Avnish get mad that he was not getting the answer she wanted. By that time, the factory had long gone out of view and Avantika had to tell Avnish.

'It's not fair,' he complained and looked for something that would be equally hard to guess.

The dinner service trolley was making its way towards them and Avantika said that they should stop playing.

'Do you think there will be sandwiches on the menu?' Avnish asked, remembering the last time they were on the same train.

'With my luck, it will be tomato rice,' Avantika replied, making a puke face. She turned to see if amma or appa had noticed and was relieved to see that appa was sleeping and amma was reading.

Appa started snoring gently, and Avantika felt mortified. Avantika imagined that the coach trembled each time appa snored. Would the bags on the luggage rack gently move each time her appa snored? What if they fell off? Now that would be terrible!

She quickly looked around to see if anyone was watching. Thankfully, he was snoring softly today, unlike at home, where Avantika and Avnish would lay wagers on whether

his snores would sound like a diesel car or a motorcycle that day. She wondered if she should go and close his mouth, but appa looked adorable sleeping peacefully. As if reading her mind, amma nudged appa and he adjusted his position, and the snoring stopped.

'Did you have fun in Coimbatore, Avanti?' amma asked, as they opened their dinner foil packs that contained lemon rice.

'I did! Did you?'

Amma nodded happily.

'I enjoy spending time with your paati and thatha. I never had brothers and sisters, so I love that your father's family is so close-knit.'

'I wish we could get to know your family too, amma.' Avantika's voice was plaintive as she made her ritual complaint.

'Avanti, you know I don't like to talk about it. Why don't you go make friends with the girl standing by the door?' amma suggested. Avantika looked up and saw the girl amma was talking about. The girl, who seemed to be the same age as her, was standing at the end of the coach, near the train door with an I-am-bored-in-this-train kind of look. 'Avni, come, let's go!'

Avantika grabbed her brother's hand and walked up to the other girl. Just as Avantika was wondering what to say, the girl spoke up.

'Where are you going?' she asked, and without waiting for them to answer, said, 'I am going to Chennai.' She seemed to be the bossy type. 'What are your names?' she asked.

Avantika couldn't help herself. 'Why don't you tell us your name instead of waiting for us to reply?'

The girl was taken aback. 'Oh! I did not mean it that way. My mom always tells me I talk too much. I am Vibha.' She stuck out her hand. Avantika took it, while Avnish kept staring at her.

'Where do you live?' Avantika asked.

'America. My grandparents live in Coimbatore. We are going to visit my cousins in Chennai. How about you?'

'Oh! Avnish and I were visiting my father's family in Coimbatore. We are going back home to Chennai. School starts in a week.'

'I have two whole months of vacation left. I am usually bored and dying to go back to school by the time it ends.'

'Me too!'

'I really like your hair. It looks beautiful!' Vibha gushed.

'Really? No one has ever said that about my hair. I usually only get complaints from amma and a bunch of folks tease me about it.'

'No way! It is so lovely. I wish my hair was curly …'

Just as Avantika blushed and searched for something appropriate to say, Vibha's mom came looking for her. They left, and Avantika suddenly felt the need to write this down in her journal.

Dear Diary,

Today, I made a new friend, Vibha. She actually thinks I have lovely hair. She is the first person to say that. I dont know how to feel about it. I mean, my hair is the kind that no matter how much you pull at it with a comb or a brush, it will always bounce right back like a spring. But imagine, she still liked it. I am happy, of course, but I also wish I had hair like amma and Avnish. Sometimes I think my birth mother must have had curly hair, which is why I have curly hair too. I wish I knew her. If only just to see how she looks.

I wonder if she has another family? Maybe I have another sister or brother? I hope she is okay. If only I could meet her once, I could show her my room and all my books. Oh! How much I would love to show her my books. Sigh! Some things you can only wish for.

The holidays have been good. Paati was the best, as always. V and V were horrible; nothing new there! Chithappa got me a new watch. Yay! I have a stack of Amar Chitra Katha books from thatha. He said that appa used to read them when he was little. I cant wait to go home and read them. I wish I could read them now, but it gives me a headache to read on the train.

Actually, writing this is also making me feel weird.

Okay, bye!

Love,

A

The light was fading, and it seemed like they had been on the train for ages. All the snacks they had were over. So, of course, even Avantika was ready to get off the train. She wondered if they would take a cab back home or an auto. She loved travelling by autorickshaws. These days she was big enough to sit with amma and appa on the auto seat. Avnish complained he always had to sit on someone's lap while she never had to. But then, Avnish always complained about something or the other. Avni could even complain if someone was nice to him, 'Why are they so nice to me? Why can't they be nice to you too?'

'We will be reaching Chennai soon,' exclaimed appa, as he suddenly woke up from his sleep. It was dark outside, and the lights inside the train were on. Other people had already started pulling out their suitcases and bags and were getting ready to get off. Avantika wished she was already in her own bed, fast asleep. She loved vacations, but she loved being home more than anything.

Back to Reality

Avantika woke to familiar sounds: traffic in the lane in front of their apartment complex, crows cawing from the terrace next to their building, sounds of clothes slapping again stone and the cacophony of maamis haggling with vegetable vendors who set up stall next to their compound. Avnish was in his bed against the wall, still fast asleep. She had fought for and gotten the bed near the window. She wanted to stay in bed longer, but she was wide awake. It was the last week of the summer holidays, and she was sure amma wouldn't mind if she slept in.

Amma worked from home. Avantika could already hear her on the phone, talking about something she had done at work before they had left for vacation. Amma called these daily meetings their scrum call and would hurry to call in every morning at seven o' clock. Appa was probably sleeping since he had to travel later in the day. He was gone most of the days, travelling to towns and villages far from the main cities. He loved to talk about how his company helped build roads and connect far-off places. Avantika wished she could go with her dad sometime, but he always kept telling her that it was tiring, dirty and most of the time there were no bathrooms on the road. She certainly could put up with being dirty and tired, but no bathrooms? She could not imagine that.

They had a lot to do in the week before school reopened. There were books to be bought and covered, uniforms to be collected from the school-mandated tailor and then there was the annual ritual of going to the book fair and getting ice creams on the way home. Avantika was impatient. Kicking off her thin bed sheet, mostly used to protect her from the stray mosquitoes that got into the room despite the sprays and the trusty plugged-in repellant, she made her way to the bathroom.

Amma was still on a call when she went to the kitchen. She saw the milk was already poured out in a cup for her and kept in the fridge. There was dosai in the hot case and chutney right next to it. Her stomach growled at the sight of food. Warming up her milk, she served herself a dosai and chutney and asked if it was okay to watch TV as she ate. Usually, amma would say no, but today she nodded and disappeared into the bedroom with her laptop. It was not often that Avantika got to watch what she wanted on TV. Avnish would fight her for the remote. She browsed through

various channels and found nothing appealing. Next, she tried Amazon Prime, but before she could decide on a show, she heard Avnish behind her, in the kitchen. Sighing, she switched off the TV, gulped her milk down and went to help him.

Amma had taught both of them to warm up milk, serve breakfast and generally be responsible for themselves. Just as she set out another plate for Avnish and sat down, amma came bustling in.

'Sorry, pattama, I had to wrap up that call before I could come to help you. Did you sleep well? Did you drink milk? We have to go to your school in the afternoon to collect your books. I will try and wrap up work for the day before then.'

Even as she asked questions, amma drew Avnish and her close and gave them a squishy hug. She ruffled Avnish's hair like she always did. Avantika knew she would not do that to her hair because it often got tangled, and it hurt when she tried to run her fingers through it. As if reading her mind, amma sighed. 'How are we going to get through the school year? Avanti, can we pretty please get your hair cut, so it is easy to manage in the morning?'

Avantika's hair grew so fast that she needed to get a haircut every few months. But this time she sat silently. She really did not want her hair to be cut. And perhaps, for the first time, it wasn't as much about her hair, as it was about the feelings inside her head.

Of late, she had been thinking a lot about her birth mother. She was convinced her birth mother must have had hair like hers. How else was her hair so different? So unruly? It was unique. She even imagined her hair to be an invisible link between her birth mother and her. Somewhat like a secret doorway.

Sometimes in class, she would swirl a lock of her hair in her finger and imagine a family full of curly-haired people. She imagined her curls growing and growing until they reached her butt!

Shaking her head, Avantika snapped out of her daydream. She would hold off saying anything to amma right now because if she did, her amma would argue with her until she gave in.

Avantika remembered the last time amma had taken her for a haircut. The kind woman at the salon was sympathetic of the unruly mess on top of her head. So, she decided to blow-dry Avantika's hair straight after the haircut. Little did she realise 'straight' and Avantika's hair didn't belong in the same sentence. Alas, her damp hair and the hot air of the hairdryer worked up so much steam that the smoke alarms went off. They all rushed out of the salon, with half of Avantika's hair curly and the other half straight. After that debacle, Avantika was not sure she could ever step foot into that salon again!

'Let's go on Sunday,' amma said and gave both of them a kiss before she disappeared into her bedroom and her work. Avantika

and Avnish knew the drill. They had to finish their breakfast, read a book or work on maths, shower and then go out to play, after telling amma where they were going. Most days it was too hot to step outside, so they waited until the evening to go to the tiny play area at the back of their apartment, where their friends usually showed up after 5 p.m.

Avantika cleared up the breakfast and wondered if she wanted to read a book or open the new jigsaw puzzle she had received for her birthday. There was a pile of books already overdue at the library. She had a bunch of books in her backpack that belonged in that pile.

Avantika's earliest memories were of her and Avnish cuddling with amma and appa on the bed and having books read to them. They had always been surrounded by books at home, and while it was natural for Avantika to pick up a book instead of running outside to play with her friends, Avnish enjoyed books being read to him. Avnish loved cricket and the fun he had outdoors. They were as different as chalk and cheese!

Or maybe she could clean up her room and surprise amma. She was waiting to wrap her books after they got them from school. She looked forward to their yearly ritual.

Avantika went back to her room, to find Avnish playing with his Rubik's cube. He almost had one side done. Puzzles didn't fascinate her the way they did Avnish. He was unusually silent. She sat next to him and held out her hand for the cube.

Avnish did not hand it over. Instead, he said, 'I heard what Vishnu and Visruth told you. It was not nice. Are you going to tell amma about it?' Avantika was not sure which conversation Avnish was talking about. He was so quiet that most times it was easy to forget he was around.

'Which conversation, Avni?' Avantika prodded.

'The one where they said mean things about us being adopted. They think I am too little to understand, but I do. I did not speak to them after that, but I don't think they even noticed.'

Avantika hugged her little brother. He was growing taller.

'It's okay, Avni. They are mean. What is the point of telling amma and appa? They will only feel bad. Chithi won't accept her sons did anything wrong. Chithappa will feel sad. Other than that, nothing will change. Anyway, we won't see them for another year at least.'

Handing over the Rubik's cube, Avnish walked to the window and sat staring outside. Not knowing how to cheer him up, Avantika handed out a chocolate bar that she had saved from the stash chithappa had given them as they were leaving Coimbatore. Miraculously, it still had not melted in the Chennai heat. It seemed to cheer him up, but now she felt terrible.

'Avni, let me help you find your new CSK T-shirt. You can wear it when we go to pick up our books from school. Do you want to show it off to your friends?' The mention of his favourite cricket team brightened Avnish, and he jumped up. 'I can get it myself,' he said, as he ran to pull out the beloved yellow tee and his black mesh shorts. He even found his matching cap at the bottom of his drawer. Cheerful now, he went to shower. While she waited, Avantika pulled out her journal.

Dear Diary,
Amma wants me to cut my hair again. This time I don't feel like cutting it. I know it is hard for amma to take care of it and I am not old enough to braid it myself, but sometimes when I look in the mirror, I feel like someone out there has hair like mine. Maybe my birth mother? I can't talk about

it to amma because I think she would feel sad.

Vibha from the train said it looks beautiful. Maybe I can learn how to care for it? Perhaps there are DIY videos I can look up. I can't wait to go to school today and meet Mythili, Sruthi and Sara. I hope they come at the same time we go there. Five more days before school reopens!

Love,

A

Hearing Avnish open the bathroom door, she quickly put her journal away and grabbed her clothes to get ready. Avnish was already out of the room and calling for amma, as she closed the door. Avantika looked at herself in the mirror. Chennai's hot, humid weather had made her hair curl up and form a frizzy circle around her head. She imagined being able to

wave a wand and transform it into something
smooth and silky, like the women's hair in the
shampoo adverts. Realising that would never
happen, she tied her hair up, stepping into the
shower. As always, her brother had left the soap
in a puddle of water. His towel was on the floor,
and his clothes were all over. Chucking them

in the laundry basket, Avantika poured almost a quarter of a bottle of shampoo onto her head and proceeded to scrub at her bunched up hair, making a mighty mess out of it. Just in case that was not enough, she added gobfuls of conditioner too and let it sit.

She sighed, wondering, why is my hair curly?

Soon, Avantika, Avnish and amma were on their way to school in a cab. They stopped at their school, then headed to the tailor and finally visited the stationery store to get school supplies. Avantika had always loved this day. She looked forward to meeting her new teachers, catching up with friends, and most importantly, finding out what books they would be reading for English. It was her favourite subject.

Amma was quiet. Avnish was chattering non-stop about his friends Sujith and Naveen. They had called earlier in the day to check when he would be at the school. All he cared about was finding out who was his class teacher and if his friends were in the same class as him.

'Amma, did you like going to school when you were little?' Avantika leaned towards her mother as she asked the question. Amma smelled like a combination of sandalwood and roses. Avantika inhaled deeply. Amma thought for a long time before she answered.

'You know, I loved school. I had lots of friends. I missed them over the summer holidays, so I always looked forward to school reopening.'

'What did you do during your summer holidays, Amma?'

Avantika was curious. Unlike appa, amma never spoke of when she was a little child or about where she had grown up. She never ever talked about her parents or family.

Just as Avantika was beginning to ask the questions she had always wanted to ask, they arrived at the school. They got off the cab and rushed through the school gates. Everything looked so familiar and new at the same time. There were plenty of parents and children running around. Avantika spied Sruthi just as Sujith came in search of Avnish. Amma clutched both their arms before they could run off.

'Let's meet your teachers before you talk to your friends,' she said, marching them towards the classrooms. Avantika was thrilled to find that her friends Sruthi, Mythili and Sara were in her class, just as Sujith turned out to be in Avnish's class. Immensely cheered after finding that out, the children ran off to the playground, while amma met and talked with the teachers and paid their fees. The last stop was the tailor's, where their clothes were ready to be picked up.

They returned home tired and happy. Avantika wanted to wrap her books with brown paper right away, but amma said they could do it together after dinner. She and Avnish watched TV while amma made their favourite dinner—poori and aloo masala. The smell of potatoes made Avantika very hungry.

After dinner, the three of them sat around the dining table, with piles of books in front of them. Amma measured and cut the paper, Avantika wrapped the books and Avnish stuck labels on them.

'Don't write anything on mine! I want to do it myself.' Avantika was dying to try the new gel pens amma had gifted her that day.

Avantika was very eager to go back to school.

Avantika's Bad Hair Day

'Wake up! Wake up!' Avnish jumped off his bed and rushed to Avantika, shaking her as he yelled. It hit her that it was the first day of school and she sprang up too. The clock by her window showed it was 6.17 a.m. The two of them took turns to brush their teeth over the sink and were done in record time.

Appa had come back home just in time for the first day of school. Avnish surprisingly cleaned up after himself well and remember to hang up his towel and put his pyjamas in the laundry basket.

'Wash your hair, Avanti,' amma reminded her from the kitchen. Not again, thought Avanti. She felt the more she resisted talking about her hair, the more amma persisted. Like yesterday, when amma had broached the 'all-important topic' of her haircut once again.

They were on the verge of declaring World War III, when appa had stepped in, waving the peace flag. He promised he would help Avanti with her hair in the mornings when he was home.

Amma finally gave in, reluctantly. Though Avantika was still smarting, amma had put the incident behind her. She had sat by Avantika's bed that night, running her fingers through her curls, trying to brush them. But her fingers got caught in the tangles instead.

Avantika had winced each time amma's fingers tugged at a strand of hair. Softening, she almost whispered, 'Okay, amma, we can get my hair cut tomorrow …' But something had made her hold on. 'Your curls look lovely,' a voice whispered in her head. There must be something she could do to learn how to care for it?

Eventually, Avantika had fallen asleep, with amma holding her hand. Appa had sat next to Avnish, telling him stories like he always did while waiting for his son to fall asleep.

Avantika loved these little back-to-school routines every year.

Now, standing under the shower, Avantika tried concentrating on the hair-wash ritual amma had been drilling into her for years. Wash, apply shampoo, rinse well, condition, use soap for the body and then wash off well, really, really well. Just as she was about to step out of the shower, she heard a knock on the door. It was amma.

'Avanti, can you please open the door?'

'Why, Amma? I washed my hair really well.'

'I know, kannu, but I just want to make sure you got all the shampoo and conditioner off your hair.'

Avantika hesitated for a moment and said, 'Okay.' She wrapped a towel around herself, pushed the doorknob open and stuck her head out the door.

Amma reached out to check her hair and said, 'Good job, kutty!' before breezing out, pulling the door behind her. Now Avantika was sure the day was off to a great start.

She wrapped her head in a thin towel, like amma had taught her, and started dressing up quickly. Her new kurta fit her well, but as she was about to put on the salwar, she realised something was off.

Where was the naada, the drawstring that held

the pants together at the hip? Had she left it in the bag the tailor had packed the clothes in? Had it fallen off the bed, where she had laid the clothes out before going to shower? Had Avnish hidden it away to play a trick on her?

Avantika searched under her pillow, beneath her bed, inside the bag her clothes had been in; she even looked inside her school bag and under Avnish's bed. It was nowhere to be seen!

It was already 8 a.m., and amma

was getting the lunch bags ready. Avantika went looking for appa, and he figured the best way to solve the problem was to use an old shoelace. Between the two, they managed to get Avantika ready just in time. Phew! That had been close.

Just as she pulled on her shoes, amma gasped. 'Avanti, your hair! We have to dry it.' A sinking feeling came over Avantika as she touched her head and felt the wet towel. She had forgotten to dry and brush her hair out! She should have agreed to get that hair cut. Even as amma blow-dried her hair and tried to run a big comb through it, it hurt. When one had naturally curly hair like Avantika, it was an everyday struggle to rake any comb-like object through it.

Avantika yelped.

Amma got tense.

Avantika grabbed the comb from her.

Appa tried to help and ended up making things worse.

Avantika gave up.

Amma walked out in a huff.

Avantika missed the bus.

It was going to be a terrible day indeed!

Appa stepped in to save the day. He dropped Avantika off to school, hugged her and promised her the day would get better.

But would it? Every bad day started with a bad hair day for her! She found herself wondering about what was in store for her through the day, as she walked inside the school gate. Grrrr … why was her hair so curly?

Avantika entered her class and found that the seat next to Sruthi had been taken. The only spot left was at the back of the class, where the boys usually sat. She did not like it there. She grudgingly put her bag down and realised she had left her lunch bag at home in hurry. Tears sprung to her eyes. Now she would be hungry all day! She had packed her favourite snack, a Rice Krispy Treat. She had seen her amma slip a note inside the bag when she thought Avantika was not looking. She knew amma had made her most favourite lunch ever. Pasta! Now she would miss it, all because of her hair.

The teacher was new and was calling out names from the attendance register.

'Avantika,' her voice rang out, and Avantika raised her hand. She could feel the back of her kurta sticking to her skin because of the water

that had seeped into it from her hair. She was wondering if she should tie up her hair when somebody hissed from behind her. When she turned to find out who was teasing her, all heads were bent.

At least the first period was English. The thought cheered her up until the teacher said they would spend the time talking about their summer vacation. She said she would call on students to come up in front of the class and talk about how they spent their holidays. Avantika ducked her head and lowered herself into her seat. Standing in front of the class and talking was the last thing she wanted to do.

Before she knew it, her name was called. Avantika froze, and when her teacher insisted, she walked up in front of the class and found she could not speak.

'I ... My family ... My brother Avnish and I ... We went to ...'

Avantika looked around, and everyone was

looking at her, waiting for her to finish her sentence. What had she planned to say? Her brain froze. She valiantly tried again.

'We … We …'

Unable to string the words together, tears welled up in her eyes, and she rushed back to her seat. Some children giggled, while her friends looked at her worriedly, wondering if she was okay. She just wished the day was over and she could go home. Lunch break was a good hour away, and she kept her head bent, listening to her friends go up and share what they had done all summer.

The next two periods went better; her hair had dried, and she was feeling a bit cheerful, when she remembered she did not have lunch. Perhaps she could share her friends' lunch? What if they had eggplant or mushrooms? She hated slimy food! She wondered how Avnish was doing. He had been looking forward to going on the school bus with her. He hated it when older boys teased him. Avantika had been his protector so far.

Even as Avantika sat wondering about everything but what her teacher was saying, the school peon was standing at the door. Avantika only noticed because the classroom had suddenly gone silent. He handed a note to their teacher and left.

'Avantika, please go to the front office. There is someone to see you,' she said.

As Avantika walked out of her class and towards the office, her heart raced.

What can it be? Is amma okay? She was mad because of the mess I made with my hair …

Can it be appa? But why would he come? He must be on his way to Salem. Is Avnish hurt?

Maybe he is already in the office? Maybe he fell off the monkey bars in the playground?

Avantika's mind swirled with scary thoughts and images of her bloody brother as she neared the office.

Avantika felt scared and anxious at the same time. This had never happened to her.

A Special Surprise

'Amma!' Avantika exclaimed, as she saw her amma standing at the front office. Amma was smiling. Avantika let out a breath she did not know she had been holding. Suddenly everything felt all right. Amma held out her arms to hug her, and Avantika felt conscious. The ladies in the front office were watching her curiously. Amma took Avantika's hand and walked out of the office. Avantika waited for her to tell her where they were going.

As soon as they reached their car in the parking lot, amma turned to her and said, 'Avanti,

I am sorry. I shouldn't have yelled at you in the morning. Will you forgive me?'

Avantika was stunned. It was rare for her to hear amma apologise. Soon they got into the car, and this time amma let her sit in the front seat. She put her seatbelt on and turned to amma.

'What are you sorry for, amma? It's okay. We both were mad, and it was my fault for forgetting my hair was still tied in a towel. But why are you not at work? Where are we going? Why isn't Avnish coming?'

The questions danced and swam around her head. Amma's eyes twinkled.

I was very upset after appa left to drop you off to school. I called my manager and said I was taking the day off. I thought about the morning and decided this was no way to start the school year. Growing up, my amma always sent me off to school in a cheerful mood because she said you learn best when you are happy. Since you also forgot your lunch at home, I decided to come to give it to you.

Besides, I feel a lot is going on in your head. Would you like to share it with your amma?

How about making this into a picnic! Let's go to the park to eat, then we'll get ice creams and head back to school. I asked for permission from your principal, and she said it is okay because it is the first day of the school year. She also made me promise I will not make a habit of it.'

Amma herself looked like a schoolgirl as she talked. Avantika had never seen her amma so relaxed and happy. Mornings and evenings were usually tense while she worked in the kitchen and held meetings as she packed lunches. In the evenings, she was hunched over her computer, catching up on everything she had missed while she sat with them for homework or set out snacks for them or helped them change. Come to think of it, all Avantika had seen her amma do was work all the time!

'Amma, why do you work so much?' The question came unprompted, and had taken amma by surprise. Amma thought a while before replying. They parked the car at the park near their home and found it strangely empty. Only a few elderly people were there. They were walking, sitting on benches, reading or sitting in groups, talking. Nobody seemed to mind them.

They picked a bench under the shade of a tree. Amma had come prepared. She spread out a mat, set out the food and sat down. As soon as Avantika sat and opened her box, amma replied, as though she had been thinking about the question all the time.

'I grew up seeing my amma work. That was all I wanted to do. At that time, not many of my aunts worked. They always seemed to think too much about buying things or doing things for themselves. I knew I wanted to make money to be independent. See, your Appa is an amazing person. He is nice because he is happy where he works. If I did not have anything to do but cook and take care of you both, I would be resentful. I work because it makes

me happy to do what I do. It makes me tired too, but I would not have it any other way.'

She looked surprised at herself for talking to Avantika like she was a grown-up. Avantika felt special.

'Amma, there is something I want to tell you too,' Avantika said, sheepishly.

'What is it, Avanti?'

'Remember how in the morning it was almost bus time, and I had forgotten to make my hair?'

'Yes, chellam. I am sorry. I should have been more patient. I was just stressed about managing work, the kitchen, your and Avnish's school work, and got a bit overwhelmed.'

'Amma, that is not what I wanted to talk about. At that moment, when I stood with a wet towel on my head and you were frustrated, and Appa did not know how to help, I wanted to cry, but not just because it was getting late for school. Because, just for a moment I thought, perhaps my birth mother would have known what to do with my hair. Maybe because she would have had hair like mine, she would have known how to care for it. I felt very sad, Amma.'

'Ammu, ammu ...'

Amma put the Rice Krispy Treats away and drew Avantika into a tight hug.

When amma finally let go, Avantika miraculously felt better. She had hesitated before telling amma about her feelings, but now, she was glad she had. Amma knew how to make her feel better.

Avantika smiled and reached for her half-eaten treat, when amma held her face with both her hands.

'Ammu, I can never know how it would have been if you had been with your birth mother. I won't pretend to know. All I know is I will do my best to be the 'best' mom to you and Avnish. I promise you, you and me both are going to learn how to do your hair.'

'Promise? Promise!'

'Now, let me finish tying your hair. I will be slow.' Amma said, reaching into her bag for the big comb.

She was. Both of them sat on the bench as amma slowly untangled her hair and tied it up in two ponytails. Impulsively, Avantika reached for amma and kissed her.

The day was perfect!

As they pulled out of their spot to go back to school, appa called. He was surprised to hear Avantika pick up the phone.

'Tell amma I need some cash from the ATM. Could she please withdraw it before the evening?'

Amma nodded as she drove and stopped at the bank on the way. Avantika had always wondered what happened in the big building near their house. She had never been inside a bank. The day was shaping up to be one big adventure. She definitely liked this and listening to all the fun things everyone did better than sitting inside the class. She wished amma and she could go outside like this every day.

A middle-aged man sat outside, with a big gun strapped on his shoulder. They walked past the metal grill and double glass doors to a room with cold air blasting from above. It felt deliciously chilled. Avantika wished she could just stand under the vent forever. Amma looked for the ATM and saw a huge line. Amma tugged at Avantika's hand, and they went inside a large room with glass partitions and the sound of clacking keyboards. There were huge monitors that flashed numbers, and there were a bunch of people sitting like they were waiting for their turn. She indicated to Avantika to sit on a bench while she took money out.

Amma pulled out her phone while she was in the line and typed away furiously. Avantika looked around. Most people seemed to be on their phones too, typing away or were sitting on the bench impatiently, waiting to be called. One elderly woman sat on the chair next to her bench. She had snowy white hair, tied in a tight bun at the back of her head. The woman seemed to be looking at amma and her too much.

She looked like the picture of the paati in her dosa book. Amma and appa had read this book to them often when they were little. It still was Avnish's favourite book. The woman in the book was plump, had a round face with circular, rimless glasses and she wore a saree in green and yellow.

Should I smile at the woman? What if she thinks I am strange? She does look sweet, though. What is the harm in a smile? The worst thing that can happen is that she will not smile back. Does it really matter?

Avantika looked up and smiled.

Where was the woman? She had been sitting right there! This really was weird.

The woman had vanished into thin air! Avantika had thought she would tell amma about the woman, but she was nowhere to be seen.

Just then, Avantika remembered she had to get back to school. She had just started worrying about missing the rest of her classes when someone shouted that the ATM in the lobby was working. Half the crowd moved to the lobby. Soon, amma and Avantika walked out with money and drove back to school. They decided to forgo the ice cream because it was getting late, and it would be more fun to have it in the evening with appa and Avnish.

Avantika walked back to school, feeling a lot happier than when she had left earlier. She was glad she was back before the recess. Oh, she had so much to talk about. She was a very lucky girl, indeed!

The Mystery Woman

The alarm rang loudly by Avantika's bedside. It was one of those old round metal clocks with fluorescent numbers and a manual wind-up key at the back. Her appa had used it when he was little. Paati had pressed it into Avantika's hands when they had left Coimbatore this time. On the first day of school, Avnish had woken Avantika before the alarm had gone off. Over the next few days, as the excitement had worn off, the alarm had proved to be useful in waking the two of them up. Avantika wished it was the weekend already. School was exciting all right, but the teachers seemed to think there was no reason to put off giving homework. Between the homework and revising what was taught in class, Avantika was so tired that she fell asleep the minute her head touched the pillow. Avnish seemed to breeze through his homework. Often, he claimed, he finished his homework at school.

That morning, Avantika had woken up with a start. Pushing away the light sheet covering her, she blinked. Where was she? She had been playing detective, spying through windows with her spy glasses; she had been dashing through the town in hot pursuit of the woman from the bank who managed to give her the slip all the time. She had just spied her in front of her home and had called out, when the alarm bell had rung.

It had all been a dream!

She chattered away while Avnish brushed his teeth, telling him all about the day before, yet again. Avnish had been mad that amma had left him at school and taken Avantika out ever since she had told him. Reminded of it again, he brushed at record speed and ran out, yelling to amma that she was unfair and he knew she loved Avantika more than him. Avantika chuckled as she brushed her teeth. It was not often that she felt like she was the chosen one.

Regardless of the love she got from her family, Avantika was often more conscious of being adopted when she saw other families that looked like each other. Her friend Sruthi looked so much like her mother that it was obvious they were amma and daughter. If only her hair was all straight and smooth like amma, then maybe they could have looked a teeny bit alike? This wish was one of those secrets no one knew, except for her journal. One night, she had written about it in a fit of frustration after someone in her school had made a rude comment on her hair.

Dear Diary,

You know how I feel about my hair, right? I really, really, really wish I had Avni's smooth, straight hair, and he had my curls. Boys can get away with so much. He could cut it short, and everyone would gush over how cute he looked. I, on the other hand, always get comments about how unruly my curls are, how amma does not know how to take care of my hair, or worse, that I have not brushed my hair—even when I have just done it.

Life is not fair!

Sometimes though, I wonder if my birth mother had hair just like me. Maybe she was worried she would not be able to take care of my hair? But why does Avni have straight hair then? We have the same mother!

Oh well! My hairy tales will never get old. Get it? Get it?
Love,
A.

Avantika showered and dressed at record speed and even reluctantly applied some coconut oil her amma had left in the bathroom, saying perhaps that would help brush her hair effortlessly. It slicked her hair down and definitely made it easier to brush. But she hated how she looked and smelled. She was worried her classmates would take to calling her something nasty. It was too late to wash her hair, so she got their school bags and made her way to the dining table. Her amma was on a work call and shushed her the minute she was about to say something.

Scowling, Avantika opened the hot case to find idlis, which she hated. She knew complaining would only make things worse, so she served herself one and saw Avnish eating his idlis, looking at amma's old phone. She made a face at him and took her idli and chutney to the living room to eat while reading a book. At least amma couldn't get mad at her for eating and reading while she was on the phone. They still had fifteen minutes before the bus came. Perhaps if she got done early, she could chat with her friends at the bus stop. Madhu usually came early with her paati.

Avantika and Avnish reached the bus stop to find they were the only ones there. Soon Sujith came, and the two boys ran around, playing tag. Avantika wished she had brought her Amar Chitra Katha along to kill time. She looked around and was surprised to see the old woman from the bank standing across the road, looking at her.

Should I wave? Should I call out? What should I call her? Woman? Paati? Old woman? Should I call Avnish and point her out to him?

By the time she looked back, deciding she would wave at her, the woman was gone!

The day at school passed uneventfully. Even the lunch break was drab. It rained, and they stayed in their classrooms, trading stories.

'Why did you not talk about your summer holidays when the teacher called you?' Sruthi asked Avantika.

'Oh! I had a horrible morning that day. You know my hair struggles, right? I washed it and forgot to dry it. I ended up missing the bus and left my lunch at home. Then the boys in the class kept calling me names. I was just so upset. I really, really wish I had hair like yours. You just have to dry and brush it and you are done! Oh! And did you know amma took me to the bank that day? I saw an old woman there who would not stop staring at me. Could it be my hair? I wondered. Then I saw her again yesterday, and before I could tell Avnish, she just disappeared!'

Just as Sruthi was beginning to ask Avantika about her outing with her mom, the bell rang, and they had to get back to class.

The bus ride home was quiet. Everybody was tired. She tried getting started on her homework, but the rocking motion made her queasy like it always did when she was in a vehicle. And she could not focus. Instead, she decided to look out the window. Just as their bus passed the bank, she saw the old, mysterious woman again. This time she did not see her.

Aha! This is it. She is new to the neighbourhood, Avantika thought as she got off the bus. She resolved that she would be friendly and wave to her if she saw her again. Avantika didn't have to wait long for that. As she got off the bus, she saw the woman across the street in front of their apartment. She waved and tugged at Avnish's shirt to point her out to him. By the time she looked back, the woman was gone. Avantika felt frustrated and a little curious.

Who was this woman? Why was she seeing her all the time? Was she some kind of illusion? Could she even be real if the only person who could see her was Avantika? She had to find out!

'What do you do when someone offers you candy or asks you for your address?' Amma's voice echoed in Avantika's ears. Ever since amma and appa had brought Avantika and Avnish home, they had started playing silly games with them.

'Tell me your address,' amma would say.

Avantika would always forget either the street or the door number.

'What is my cell phone number?' appa would ask.

By the time Avantika was eight, she knew the house address and telephone number by heart. She also knew that she was not to share this with anyone she did not know.

'What do you do if someone touches your private parts?' amma would ask, as she helped Avantika get changed into her pyjamas for bed.

'Scream as loud as I can and run!' Avantika would say. Avnish and Avantika would take turns showing how she should scream. They usually laughed as they pretend-screamed, but as they brushed their teeth themselves and got ready to sleep, amma would hold both of them close and remind them to never talk to strangers, never accept candy or gifts from people they did not know and never ever get into a vehicle with a stranger, even if they knew the person, unless of course amma or appa asked them to.

Suddenly everything amma and appa had told her about stranger danger came to Avantika's mind. She should be careful, she thought. She would keep her eyes peeled for this new paati and be very, very careful.

They reached home, and Rukmini akka opened the door for them. She had been away to visit family in her native place and had just returned after a long time. She came every evening to help amma cut vegetables, make rotis and some subzis. She also stayed with them until amma came home when she went to the office once or twice a week.

Recently amma had been going to office more often, relying on Rukmini akka to be there for them. Avantika and Avnish loved her.

After they got back from school, Rukmini akka helped them get their bags off, picked up their socks and uniforms and started the washer load for the day. She also got milk and biscuits for them as they worked on their homework.

Some days akka oiled Avantika's hair, brushed it evenly without causing her pain and braided it into tight braids that she wore to school the next day. Avantika looked forward to these evenings as she would read, while Rukmini akka did what she did well—braid her hair.

Rukmini akka had a son, Shankar, the same age as Avnish. Sometimes, if she was done with her work early, she would take the three of them to the park down the road, where Avantika and amma had had their picnic on the first day of the school year. Both children looked forward to the days they could go to the park.

That day was their lucky day. Rukmini akka finished her work early and asked them to get ready to go to the park. The three of them walked to the park and found it crowded. Avnish found his friends there and ran off to play, with Rukmini akka trailing after him.

'Rukmini akka, I will sit on this bench and read. I don't feel like playing on the swings or slide. Also, none of my friends is here. Is it okay? I have amma's old phone with me, and I have your number if I need to call you. I promise to be careful. You can see me here from the play area.'

Avantika looked at Rukmini akka with what she thought were puppy eyes. Akka gave her consent.

'Stay right here paapa. I have to be with Avnish thambi.'

Avantika nodded. Rukmini akka left.

Avantika settled down on the bench. There will be enough light for an hour, she thought. She was engrossed in the book when suddenly she felt she was being watched. She looked around and saw no one. She tried to read, but the nagging feeling returned, and she closed the book and clutched her phone tightly. Just as she thought perhaps her nerves were on edge because of seeing the old woman from the bank, she really saw her. In the few minutes Avantika had bent to put her book into her bag, the woman had actually come and sat next to her! Avantika was not sure if she should run or confront her. Before she could decide, the woman spoke.

'What is your name? My name is Saraswathy. I live on the road next to your apartment complex. Sorry if I have been staring at you. You look like someone I know.' She spoke in a soft voice and seemed to be kind.

Avantika did not relax, though. She had heard enough stories from her amma and friends about how children got kidnapped for stopping and speaking to strangers. She looked to see if Rukmini akka was nearby.

Should she run? She could run faster than the woman. Should she ask her what she was doing following her around? Avantika was feeling conflicted. She stood at a safe distance, mulling over what to do.

Saraswathy seemed to sense Avantika's dilemma. She held out her hands simply, as if to say, I am not dangerous. She opened her bag and showed Avantika that all she had was a purse and a book.

Avantika relaxed enough to breathe but held on to her phone and looked for Rukmini akka every once in a while. Her curiosity got the better of her.

'My name is Avantika. Who do I remind you of?' she asked boldly.

'I will tell you another day. But tell me about the book you are reading,' the old woman said.

Talking about books seemed harmless, so Avantika smiled and sat on the bench. She told her all about the *Harry Potter* series she had

just started reading. Her voice rang out with excitement when she found that the old woman helped at the library in a school and knew all about the series. She had been badgering her amma and appa to read with her, but they couldn't always make time. They all mostly ended up watching movies together.

Suddenly Saraswathy, who insisted that Avantika call her paati instead of auntie, said she had to leave and got up and left.

'Paapa, let's go! It is getting late. I still need to fold clothes and put them away before I leave. You and thambi have to finish your homework too.' Rukmini akka and Avnish waited impatiently for Avantika to grab her bag and walk with them.

'Rukmini akka, there is a paati who keeps following me around. I saw her at the bank, then again at the bus stop, and today at the park. She even sat on the same bench I was sitting on. And, just like that, she got up and left!'

'Paapa, you always like to tell stories. Maybe one day you will become a great writer and write books like the ones you read.' Rukmini akka's eyes twinkled as she said this.

'Akka, you always like adventures and keep making up stories. I don't believe you,' Avnish declared.

Avantika walked home in a daze and thought she would not say anything to anyone if this was how they were all going to treat her. She was no longer a child. She knew what she was saying. The woman was real, and that was that!

The Secret Hideaway

It had been an eventful few weeks. Avantika settled in at school, but the thing she most looked forward to were the evenings. Most days, Rukmini akka, Avnish and she walked down to the park. Avantika looked forward to the days she could discuss her favourite *Harry Potter* book with Saraswathy paati. They made an unlikely pair, one young and spritely and the other wise, with owl-like glasses. They had one thing in common though, wisps of coiled, curly hair that framed their face.

Even though it had only been a few days, Avantika felt a connection with paati that she could not put in words. She thought of her like Dumbledore, someone benevolent and out of reach, yet a presence she could not ignore.

Avantika liked Saraswathy paati's warm presence in her life. She remembered the photographs amma showed her of the orphanage from where they came. The pictures always featured an older woman who held Avantika. She looked nothing like paati, but she had that same kind look on her face.

Amma often talked to her about the first few months after Avnish and she had come home from the orphanage.

'You would cry for no reason and appa would carry you and walk all around the house while I took care of Avnish. He was such a small baby and would mostly eat and sleep. You, on the other hand, made sure everyone around gave you their attention …'

Now Avantika wondered if she had cried so much because she had missed the paati at the orphanage.

Of late, Avantika had taken to slacking off in class. She would be looking at the teacher and the board, but her mind would be far away, in a magical land where elves and spells were aplenty. How she wished she would get a letter from Hogwarts and go away! She had imagined it in her head so many times.

'Avanti, you have a letter. It has a strange-looking seal on it ...'

'Avantika ...'

'Avantika ...'

The voice seemed too close and real to be in her head. Shaking herself from her daydream, she found her teacher calling out to her, exasperation writ large on her face.

'Do you want me to send a note home, missy? If I find you daydreaming one more time, I will send you to the principal's office ...'

The teacher's threat hung in the air while Avantika resolved to focus on what was happening around her. She could hear Sruthi and Mythili giggling and knew they would start teasing her again about imaginary crushes.

Avantika was relieved when the day was over and she was on the bus home.

The evenings they did not go to the park, Avantika wrote in her journal. Reading and writing were a way for her to put away her feelings in a safe place, locked and secure. Writing helped her feel light and happy. She wrote about meeting Saraswathy paati, and though she knew it wasn't the right thing to do, it felt so right. She wrote about her hair, and how it made her feel different, distinct, a veritable Medusa in a house filled with sleek-haired people. She wrote about how it felt not to fit in with anyone—at home, in school, amongst cousins. She felt confused because she knew everyone loved her, but then why did she feel this way?

Avantika looked forward to the days Rukmini akka was home in the evenings. She would beg Rukmini akka to finish work early so they could go to the park. Avnish would tease her that she was looking forward to meeting her imaginary friend. Avantika brushed away the teasing and remembered to pack her books with her. Sometimes she would pack an extra snack for paati. It was good having a friend who understood her love for reading and shared the joys of talking about characters as if they were real.

As they walked into the park, Avnish was excited to see his friend Sujith there. Rukmini akka and Sujith's paati chatted while they watched the children play. Avantika was disappointed not to find her friend at the usual spot. She wondered if she would show up late, like she sometimes did. She also looked at the base of the tree, they called their tree, next to the bench. Paati had shown her a hiding spot, a little hollow that was covered with a wild plant growing at the base.

'It can be our secret hiding place,' she had said, showing Avantika how to leave things wrapped in a plastic bag. One day Avantika had found a note from Saraswathy paati, stating she was going out of town and would be back the following week. One time she had found a book, an old dog-eared copy of *The Little Prince*.

Avantika kept meaning to leave something for her friend but had never had a chance. That day she found the perfect opportunity. She ripped out a page from the journal she would carry with her all the time. She started writing.

Dear Paati,

I was hoping to see you here today. I had a good day at school. Well, almost. I got caught in class for daydreaming. Sometimes it is hard for me to stop thinking about the books we talk about. I wish that were all we did in school. I find maths and science boring! History and geography are not so bad. At least we get to read about people and places. I wonder what use people have for maths, especially when we can use calculators and computers to do our work.

I hope I will see you the next time I am in the park. Amma has been very tense this week. She says her project is not going well. She often yells at us because she is frustrated. I am not sure what to do. I think it is unfair of her to take her anger at something else out on us. However, I cannot tell her that. Or should I?

Appa keeps travelling, and sometimes I hope that he can be like other dads and work in Chennai. That way amma won't have to do everything. Then maybe she will be happy and not as angry.

I have only ever heard her talk about

her childhood once and she sounded so happy and relaxed when she did. I wish her family would speak to her. She never talks about them.

Everybody needs someone to listen to them, right?

Sometimes I wonder what happened between my amma and her amma. It is not like she was adopted or left in an orphanage like Avnish and I were. Amma says she really loved school and when she talks about her amma she looks so happy. I wish she would tell me what happened. Oh well, here I go rambling again.

I am glad we are friends.

Avantika

PS: I must tell you that I was afraid you were evil when I first saw you staring at amma and me at the bank. I hope it is okay for me to tell you that.

Avantika looked around in her bag to find something to wrap her letter in to keep it from getting wet. Finding nothing, she decided to make an envelope out of another sheet and wrap the message in it. Just as she was done putting the letter in the hollow, she heard Avnish's voice and quickly straightened up. Gathering her things, she walked towards Rukmini akka and Avnish before they could see what she was doing.

'You look pleased with yourself, miss; what are you up to?' Rukmini akka asked. She always read Avantika better than anyone else.

'Nothing.'

'Nothing?'

Avantika decided it was better to change the topic before akka made her spill everything out. Avantika never could keep a secret. It was amazing that she had kept her friend a secret from everyone for so long. Even when Avnish had caught her reading *The Little Prince* and wanted to know who had given it to her, she had

said that it was from the library and turned over to face the window.

They reached home and to their delight, saw both amma and appa at home. It always was a good time when appa was back. Avantika flew into his arms.

'Appa, I wish you would never have to travel again,' she whispered when she closed her eyes that night.

Avantika Learns to Braid

That day had been a particularly hard day for Avantika. Appa was away (as always). Amma had been too busy even to try to fix her hair. Avnish had been bratty, hiding her things. She had found her bag with the journal on the bed instead of the study table drawer, where she usually kept it. Her uniform was wet because it had rained and all of them had forgotten to remove the clothes from the clothesline last night. Amma had done her best to iron it so it would be partially dry, but it smelt like a wet dog.

She had managed to gather her messy locks into a ponytail, but it looked like she had just woken up and gotten to school. She was sure her teacher would remark on it because her hair looked somewhat like a mop that had been connected to an electric plug, with its bristles standing in attention. While she was upset that her teacher usually called attention to things like clothes and hair, it bothered her more when they pulled her aside to advise or tell her that she needed to ask her mother to do better.

Her friends, too were acting strangely these days. It probably had to do with how she often smiled in the middle of a conversation, and she had no idea what they were talking about because she was thinking about something else. They were sure she had a crush on some boy that she wasn't telling them about. That was all her friends could think of these days.

Avantika did not know whether to be upset or laugh at them. She had taken to eating her lunch by herself at lunchtime, burying her nose in a book like she always did. She wondered if it was time to get glasses because she had trouble holding the book at arm's length, like her amma insisted she does. She would hear an earful about how she was reading all the time, and if only she spent a fraction of that time on actual schoolwork, she could get good grades.

Somehow, when amma lectured her, Avantika felt like she was doing so just because she had to. It was not like when appa asked her to study. Then she knew he meant what he said. He would put her books away and sit with her to help her with her homework or quiz her on what had happened in class in each subject. Avnish would hang on his back and make faces at her, but overall it was always better when appa was around.

The bus came late, and the roads were muddy from the rain. The morning sky reflected her mood—it was steely grey, with dark clouds

hovering above. Everybody seemed to be in a bad mood. Avantika trudged into class, only to find that the last bench was again the only bench available for her to sit. These days she seemed to prefer it though. She put her bag down and looked at the board, only to find there was a pop quiz going on. Hoping to score a passing grade, Avantika pulled out her rough-work notebook in case she had to work out an answer.

The rest of the day went predictably, and she felt better when the sun came out around noon. She had been looking forward to going to the park in the evening and had been sure it would not happen because of the rain. Now the thought of being able to see paati after a long time was enough to put a spring in her step. She even made an effort to listen to her friends and join in the conversation. Even though the conversations at school were so far removed from what she really wanted to discuss—*Harry Potter*—she realised she did enjoy their company, after all.

Thankfully Rukmini akka was already there when they reached home, and she was almost done with her chores for the day. Avantika completed her homework as fast as she could and even helped Avnish with his so they could go out.

Finally, they set out, and Avantika found that their usual spot had already been taken by a mother and her child. She stood nearby and hopped from foot to foot impatiently, hoping they would take her cue and find another spot to sit. Eventually, she gave up and moved to another bench. She would have to go back a little later to see if the letter she had left for paati was gone or was still there.

Just as she started walking to let Rukmini akka know that she would be sitting at a different bench, further away, she spotted paati. Her heart skipped a beat. She rushed towards her like a long-lost friend. Paati seemed just as delighted to see her. They turned back and found their old seat empty and walked back there, catching up on everything they had missed over a couple of weeks.

'I got your letter. It was lovely!' paati said affectionately. 'There was a time when I used to write long letters. I haven't written many over the past few years,' she said wistfully.

'Why, Paati?' Avantika wanted to know.

'Oh! There is no one to write to these days.'

'Well! You have me now.'

'Yes! I do,' said paati and tried to ruffle Avantika's hair lovingly. 'You really need to get your hair brushed ...' said paati, as she looked critically at Avantika's hair. As they sat down on the bench, paati did something out of the ordinary. She let her hair down, and it came cascading down her back in waves. Just as she did that, the tiny wisps of hair around her face curled up and formed a halo just like Avantika's did. For a moment, Avantika felt a strong feeling of love envelop her. She felt a sense of connection to this strange lady, with hair just like her own! Avantika's mind raced. Perhaps her birth mother and grandmother had hair like hers? Was that why she felt a connection to this paati? If only she really were her paati ...

Shaking her head, as if to clear her thoughts away, Avantika gazed with longing at paati's hair. It indeed was magnificent: thick waves cascaded down her back, tiny wisps seemed to trap the evening sun in their grey strands. For all she knew, paati could be a warrior character in her Amar Chitra Katha books, the way she looked now.

Did Avantika ever look like that to another person? Was that what Vibha had meant when she said her curls were gorgeous? She deliberated.

Noticing Avantika lost in thought, paati asked her to put the books away. She declared that she was going to teach Avantika how to braid her hair. She dug around in her bag and fished out a big brush and a wide-toothed comb. Avantika was happy to see it was clean.

As if reading her mind, paati said, 'I keep this as a spare in this bag. The ones I use regularly are at home. Is it okay if I use this to brush your hair?'

Avantika looked around to see if anyone was watching and quickly nodded yes when she saw there was no one. She sat facing away and prepared herself for the pain that would ensue. But paati's touch was soft, and the brush did not pull at her hair like it did when she brushed her hair. The brush seemed to bend and move with the hair. After what seemed like a long time, paati finished brushing and gave instructions as she braided Avantika's hair.

'Divide your hair into three parts. Now put the first section over the second. Then the third over the second. Repeat until you reach the end …' She sounded like the people in the DIY videos on YouTube that Avnish loved to watch. And though she didn't even glance at them at home, here she was now, listening in rapt attention.

Paati kept repeating the instructions until she had tied up Avantika's hair in two thick braids on either side of her head. Now you try it on my hair, she said, thrusting the brush and comb into Avantika's hands. Avantika felt super weird. It was one thing to be friends with someone she barely knew, but to touch their hair felt like she was crossing some boundary. Paati sensed she was hesitating and gently reminded her that if she did not practise, she would not learn. That was all Avantika needed to hear.

How wonderful it would be if she could do her hair without help! Avantika thought wistfully.

She tried to remember what paati had done and started tentatively. It took a few tries before she got the rhythm right, but she eventually managed a full braid, even if it was lopsided, with uneven locks of hair. Avantika watched as paati deftly undid what she had done, plaited her hair quickly and wrapped it into a bun at the back of her head.

'I will see you again,' she said before disappearing.

Avantika turned, expecting to see Rukmini akka or Avnish, but there was no one. Why did paati leave so suddenly? She wondered. She fingered her braid and wondered if she should let her hair loose. Even as she was deciding upon it, she heard Rukmini akka's voice and walked towards her.

It was like no one noticed that she had a different hairstyle from when she had entered the park. Avnish said nothing. Rukmini akka was talking to someone on her phone and did not notice. Amma came home just as Avantika was brushing her teeth before bed. She kissed her absently on her cheek, tucked her into bed and went to Avnish.

Just like that, Avantika realised she could practise braiding her hair at home, and no one would be the wiser. She wished she had a doll like some of her friends did, so she could try it on someone other than herself. Then she fell into a deep sleep, dreaming of curly-haired dolls and people who looked like her.

The Cat's Out of the Bag

It was a Friday evening. Avantika had no homework. Rukmini akka was taking longer than usual to finish up her chores. Avantika was impatient. She hopped on one foot. She fiddled with the front doorknob. She was raring to go out. Even Avnish started getting annoyed with her impatience.

'All you ever do is sit on a bench and read at the park. Why can't you do it at home?'

Before she could help herself, it slipped out. Her little secret of many months was finally out in the open!

'Paati will be there. We have the most fun conversations. She even taught me to braid. Haven't you noticed?' She swung her head from side to side. Her oddly shaped plaits moved in synchrony. Avnish was not sure if he should believe her.

'Your imaginary paati is real? I will believe you when I see her,' he said and rushed to the phone when it rang.

'Rukmini akka, Sujith's paati is taking him to the park, can I pretty please go with him?' he pleaded.

'Ayyo paapa, I am done, I will take you both in a minute. Get ready and put your shoes on,' Rukmini akka said, as she bustled out of the kitchen, a huge trash bag in hand.

Akka dropped the bag in the apartment dumpster, washed her hands and proceeded to walk slightly behind Avantika and Avnish. Avnish strained to walk fast so he could catch up with his friend.

They reached the park, and surprisingly it was not crowded for an evening.

Sujith was waiting for Avnish by the monkey bars. Rukmini akka sat nearby, keeping an eye on them, while Avantika walked to her favourite spot. Paati was already there. She waved and held out yet another book. This time it was a favourite tale, one that their Coimbatore paati had told Avantika and Avnish many times over.

Vikram and Betaal, the cover read. Avantika could not wait to dig into it.

Avantika began unprompted, talking about her school, her friends, her family and everything under the sun. She had barely finished telling paati how appa should be home that night when she spied the telltale teal blue of their old Maruti 800 on the road, heading home.

'Amma is already home! I wonder if she will come looking for us at the park. Perhaps you could meet her Paati,' she said and turned to look at her friend.

WHY IS MY HAIR CURLY?

Paati suddenly looked off-colour. She dabbed her forehead with the edge of her saree and gathered her things.

'I think I will head home today. You enjoy your weekend, Avantika. I will see you next week.'

She practically rushed out of the park and hurried along the road.

Just as Avantika had predicted, amma came looking for them in a few minutes. She looked preoccupied.

'Where is Avni? Let's go, Avanti.'

'Amma, there is something I have to tell you. Something I should have told you a long time ago. Do you remember ...'

Amma cut her off midway. 'Avanti, can we talk about whatever it is on our way? I just need to go home.'

'Amma! You never listen to me when I talk. Will you listen to me if I tell you I made friends with an unknown Paati?!'

Now she definitely had amma's attention. She

stopped, turned to face Avantika and lowered her voice.

'What Paati? You know appa and I have told you never to talk to strangers—where is Rukmini? She was supposed to keep an eye on both of you …'

Avantika held out the book paati had given her. The sight of the book stopped amma in her tracks, and she held out her hand for it.

'Let me see it.' Amma looked anxious as she took it from her. She flipped it from the front cover to the back, inspecting it as one would look at something familiar. 'Let's go get Avnish and go home. I am tired, kannamma. Let's talk about your friend at home.'

Avantika and amma headed out for the swings and tried convincing Avnish to go home with them. He really wanted to stay because Sujith was not going back yet. Rukmini akka promised to stay awhile and bring him back.

'Amma, why are you so silent? Are you okay?' Avantika asked. It was like amma was unable to hear her.

Was amma angry with her?

Did amma know Saraswathy paati?

Both Avantika and paati had curly hair; maybe they were related? How cool would that be!

Avantika turned to look at her amma and realised amma did not look angry or sad. She seemed puzzled and worried.

They reached home, and Avantika reached out to get her book from amma.

Amma held her close and asked her to repeat how she had met paati and what other things paati had given her so far. Avantika was surprised that amma did not scold her for talking to strangers or taking things from them.

She started at the beginning, right from when she had seen the paati staring at amma and her at the bank and ended with the day's events.

'Wait, amma. Let me get everything she gave me.'

Avantika ran to her room, feeling relieved that she no longer had to carry her secret. The box under her bed was heavy, laden with the books and trinkets she had collected over the past few weeks.

She half expected amma to scold her, but nothing happened.

Amma reverently touched the books, opened them and put them away. She even laughed when she saw the little bead bracelet that had the letter 'R' engraved in it.

The emotions on amma's face were a mixture of disbelief and happiness. It was almost like amma was playing some movie in her head.

'Amma, you are not upset, are you?'

'No kannu, I am not. Can you run and watch some TV? There is something I have to do.'

With that, she left abruptly.

Avantika was convinced now—she had done something really, really wrong. It was scary when amma shouted at her for mistakes but more terrifying when she was silent. Avantika decided against watching TV and went to her room. She pulled out her journal like she did whenever she was not sure how to feel.

Dear Diary,
Did I do something wrong? Why is amma acting so strange? I wish she would talk or even scold me like she sometimes does.
   Love,
   A

Even words failed her today, and Avantika closed her journal.

It felt like a long time before Avnish and Rukmini akka reached home. Amma was still not out of her room. Avantika was not sure if she should go check in on her. Luckily for her, appa reached home. He asked for amma and Avantika poured out the story to him. 'What was the lady's name again?' he asked. 'Saraswathy?' he repeated.

Now appa was being just as mysterious as amma. He looked puzzled, his brows arching over his eyes the way they did when he worked on crosswords. However, he didn't look as shaken as amma. That made Avantika feel a little better.

He looked around, put his bag away, peered into the kitchen and declared he would get food from outside for all of them. He then said they could watch TV.

Avantika knew something was terribly wrong. Amma and appa both wanted them to watch TV. It was something unheard of. Something certainly was not okay!

Watching TV felt like punishment to Avantika but Avnish seemed unbothered by everything happening around him. He gladly switched to videos of Beyblades, something that Avantika did not care for.

Avantika finally decided to be brave and talk to amma. She reached her amma and appa's bedroom to find it shut from inside. She could hear whispers, though. It sounded like amma was crying and appa was consoling her.

Dear God! What have I done? Avantika questioned herself. Just as she was about to walk back to her room, amma came out clutching an envelope.

She knelt in front of Avantika.

'Avanti, this may seem strange to you. I believe that you do have a friend. I did see her on my way to the park. I am not angry with you. We will talk about this another day. But I want you to do me a favour. I want you to give this letter to your friend paati when you see her next. I also want you to invite her home and tell her that your amma and appa would love to meet her. Can you do that for me?'

Wordlessly, Avantika took the letter from amma. It was sealed. Confusion reigned supreme in her head. Clearly, there was more to the story. Who was this paati? What was this all about? If amma believed her, why weren't they meeting paati together? Why were her parents being so secretive? This definitely seemed very strange!

That night Avantika had trouble sleeping, even after amma sat with her a long time, patting her head and telling her everything was okay. Avantika was very tempted to open the envelope and see what was inside. She wondered if it would solve the mystery. But she remembered her amma's sad face and decided she had to wait.

Each day she went to the park but did not see her friend. She asked amma if she could leave the letter in the tree hollow.

'You have a secret hiding place?' Amma seemed incredulous. 'No, just wait until you see your paati to give it to her.'

A couple of weeks passed before Avantika saw Saraswathy paati again. Paati seemed older than before.

'Why did you not come all these days? I missed you! I have been waiting for you,' Avantika said, as she ran to her.

'I have been unwell, child. I came to say bye to you today. I will be travelling for a while.'

'Paati, I have something for you from my Amma. She asked me to give this letter to you.'

Avantika handed the letter to her.

'Paati, Amma says she saw you. She asked me to tell you to come home. She and Appa really would love for you to visit us. You know where we live, right?'

Avantika looked expectantly at paati. Avnish joined them, and paati looked from him to Avantika.

'I can't promise, Avantika. Let me think it over.'

Paati looked really old all of a sudden. The wrinkles on her face stood out. She seemed to shrink in height. Avantika wondered if she would just sit down on the bench. Paati seemed tired, the way one does when one is carrying a massive weight on one's head.

I know how it is to carry a heavy load on the head … thought Avantika.

Paati ruffled Avnish's hair and dug in her bag for the toffees she always carried. She handed a fistful to each and hugged them before she turned and left.

Feeling sad, Avantika and Avnish went home with Rukmini akka. Avnish said he finally believed Avantika.

'She looked like a nice Paati. Why did you not call me before to meet her?' he demanded.

Avantika did not feel like talking to anyone. She felt sad. And she knew that feeling well. The kind of feeling that made her feel empty inside. The thought of not seeing her friend again made her want to cry.

She hid away in her room for most of the evening, not wanting to tell amma that paati may not come to visit them after all. Amma reached home early. Even appa was home today. It was almost time for dinner when the doorbell rang. Avantika hoped it was paati. She was right!

Paati stood at their door with a bag in hand.

We Are a Happy Family

Avantika rushed to hug her.
Amma kept looking at paati, but she couldn't utter a word.

'Ulla vaango, please come,' appa said, asking paati inside.

'I am so happy you came. Please take a seat,' said appa, gesturing towards the sofa where they usually sat and watched TV.

Paati came inside but did not say anything. She handed a bag over to Avnish. Amma still did not say anything. Avantika felt like a tennis ball, her head turning between amma and paati, waiting for someone to say something.

Suddenly amma walked over and hugged paati. They both were crying. Appa held Avantika's hand. Avnish was still blissfully rummaging through the bag, pulling out the toys and books.

Avantika wished they would talk, so she could finally know the answers to the questions that had been spinning in her head all evening.

What was in the letter amma had written to paati?

Why were they crying?

Why had amma not scolded her at all?

Why was appa silent?

Who *is* paati?

The questions came at her like a tsunami, each wave bigger and more powerful than the one before.

'Avanti, come here,' amma said, and Avantika ran to join her and paati.

'She is your paati. She is my amma.'

'Really! But she is so nice! Why did you both not talk to each other? Why did we miss out on knowing her for all these years? It's not fair, Amma.'

All of them laughed on hearing Avantika burst out in indignation.

Paati gathered Avantika and Avnish in her lap.

'A long time ago, your Amma came to me and told me she loved your Appa. I was hurt that your Amma did not include me in her decision. I behaved like a child would and threw a tantrum and moved to a different city. The fault is all mine …'

Paati then looked up at Avantika's amma and appa.

'Radha, maapilai, you must forgive me. I am older and wiser now and have two beautiful grandchildren whom I would like to have in my life.'

Appa went and sat next to paati. He took her hand in his.

'Amma, I know you wanted Radha's best. I will be happy if you are part of our family now. I know Avantika already calls you Paati. Will you allow me to call you Amma too?'

Paati nodded.

The rest of the evening went by, with paati

joining them for dinner. She did not say much but kept looking at amma all the time. Avantika found it strange to have someone call her amma by name or look at her like that.

Suddenly, Avantika realised that amma and paati had different hair.

'I have hair like Paati's!' she declared.

'I know,' chorused Paati and amma.

As if suddenly remembering something, amma looked at paati and told her, 'You know Avnish and Avantika are adopted, right? We adopted them when they were little.'

'I know. Avanti once mentioned something in a letter she wrote to me. But then, knowing you, it is not surprising. You always were one to go against the crowd.'

Paati and amma smiled knowingly. It was so good to see everyone happy.

'I am so happy you both adopted Avantika and Avnish. They are adorable, and the best grandchildren I could hope for. I have gotten to know Avantika a little, and I have all the time in the world to get to know Avnish now!' paati said.

It was long past Avantika's bedtime when, paati said she had to go home. Amma and appa insisted that she stay the night.

'I live in the next street next to Sujith and his paati's place. It is not too far. I will be back tomorrow for my grandchildren,' she said, her eyes twinkling.

Appa dropped her home and came back to tuck Avantika and Avnish in bed. Even though Avantika thought she could never sleep from all the excitement, she was asleep the minute her head touched the pillow. She dreamt of paati braiding her hair. It made her smile.

It Is Okay To Be Different

Avantika was excited to go to school. She had been daydreaming in class. She had not been doing well in tests. Her friends thought she was strange. Today she could tell them all that she had a new paati!

At school, Avantika could not stop smiling the entire day. She was attentive in class. She actually answered when her teachers called out to her. She still read when she ate her lunch but remembered to put her book away when someone spoke to her. Her world felt all right again. She even managed to walk up to the front of her class when her teacher called out to ask if anyone knew what an extempore speech was.

As she walked to the front of the classroom, she wondered what she should speak about, and it came to her. Her hair, of course! What else had been weighing on her so much all the time?

'Good morning all!' she began with confidence.

'My hair and I have had a complicated relationship. Sometimes I feel it is beautiful. Other days, I wish it would disappear magically and I would have hair like my Amma—straight and smooth. Sometimes I want to cut it short because it makes amma happy. Other days, I want it long like Rapunzel. Believe me, it's not easy not knowing why my hair is curly.

Some of you may already know my brother and I are adopted. Being adopted means you are always aware of being different. That my hair is so different from the rest of my family made me focus on it so much more. I kept thinking if only my hair was different, say like Sruthi's, then all my problems would go away. I would fit right in. No one would tease me about it. And, I wouldn't have people try to put pencils through my hair or call me 'Saibaba' or 'Medusa'.

Today, though, I think I've finally made peace with my hair. It is who I am.

Whether curly, unruly, messy or gorgeous, as some people seem to think, this is what I have. This is who I am. Today I am accepting who I am, the way I am.'

Avantika beamed, knowing for once that she had not stuttered, she had actually said what she wanted to say and, even if only she thought so herself, had done well!

Her class seemed to agree, because everyone clapped hard, and her teacher clapped the hardest of them all!

When she and Avnish reached home in the evening, Rukmini akka was there, but so was

paati. Avnish wondered if they would no longer go to the park because Avantika wanted to stay home with paati. 'Now that you have your Paati, you no longer need me,' Rukmini teased Avantika, as she went out with Avnish.

As paati oiled and braided Avantika's hair neatly, Avantika said happily, 'I will never have to cut my hair again!'

'Why? Do you want long hair?' asked paati.

Avantika thought for a long time before answering.

'I don't know. I met someone on the train who said my hair looks beautiful. I feel out of place at home because everyone else has straight hair. Some days I want to chop it all off. Other days I feel like maybe I have hair like my birth mother and I don't want to get it cut. I really don't know …'

Paati thought for a while before replying.

'You know, when your amma was a little girl, she always wanted to have her hair long. Your thatha died a long time ago, and I had to work to support your amma and myself. So, I would make her get a haircut to make it easier for me in the mornings. She never would say anything. I discovered that she hated cutting her hair when I found one of her diaries in her room, after she went to college. If I had known earlier, I would have let her grow it out. It is just hair. If cutting your hair bothers you, you should talk to amma; maybe she will understand. If you don't say why your hair matters to you, how will she know?'

Avantika thought about what paati had said. It was true. How would amma know how she felt if she didn't tell her? She was also glad that her amma hadn't read her journal. She would remember to pack her journals with her when she went to college.

That night, after amma came home from work, Avantika went up to her and said she wanted to talk about her hair.

Amma gathered her in her lap and gave her full attention.

'Amma, I have been thinking and talking to paati about my hair and how I feel about cutting it. She is right. It is just hair. It will grow back. Can we go this weekend and get it cut so that I can brush it myself?'

'Are you sure, chellam? Now that you can make braids yourself and you have paati to help you, you can let it grow if you want. You know, I wanted to have long hair when I was growing up, but my Amma, your Paati, would always make me wear it short. You should do what you want. I am glad you came and talked to me though.'

'It's okay, amma. I thought a haircut meant I would end up losing something my birth mother gave me. But I realise that, you have straight hair while paati has curly hair like me. I was perhaps wrong linking my hair to my birth mother's. It's just hair. It will grow back. Let's get it cut. To be honest, it is a lot of work in the mornings when I would rather read a book.'

Amma smiled at Avantika.

ACKNOWLEDGEMENTS

This book would not have been possible without Vidhi Bhargava, who reached out to me with the idea of a children's book. Without her encouragement, patience and positivity, I would have not been a published author.

If words make a story, pictures bring them to life. I owe Niloufer Wadia my gratitude for bringing the characters in my head to life and making it easier for the little readers to connect to their friends from the book.

 I owe a deep debt of gratitude to Isha Muthu, my alpha reader, for her vote of confidence and the insightful comments on the draft manuscript. She will forever be the child who inspired Avantika.

To my friends Srividya Srinivasan, Suman Murali, Chithra Jeyaram, Lakshmi Gopal, Priya Muthu, Lorraine Storms and Jean Burke-Spraker, I thank you for the endless hours of support, sisterhood and a belief in my abilities that kept me going.

To Shymol Chambachan, Shailaja Vishwanath, Shweta Ganesh Kumar and the countless friends and family members who are rooting and cheering me on, my heartfelt thank you.

To the many adoptees voices including Sandy Blais, Rhonda Roorda, Jessenia Parmer and Anne Heffron, I owe a debt of gratitude for helping shape my views on adoption.

To fellow adoptive parents including Susan Silverman, Nico Opper, Lori Holden, Maggie Rangan, Sangitha Krishnamurthi, Nancy Leschke, Sharon Van Epps, Shankari Arcot, Mahasweta Bag, thank you for being my tribe.

To the mother of my twins, Brandy Stein, I owe my happiness to you.

To my children Anjali, Meghna and Sahana; I hope someday you are proud of Amma. I am infinitely proud of being your amma.

To Narayanan, I am forever grateful for the unconditional acceptance and support through any path I have chosen in life.

To Amma, for being there, always!

To Appa, because you believed in me long before anyone else did. I miss you.

Glossary

Amma: Mother

Appa: Father

Paati: Grandmother

Thatha: Grandfather

Chithappa: Father's younger brother

Chithi: Wife of father's younger brother/mother's younger sister

Vadaam: Sun-dried rice crisps which are fried to make a snack

Palapazham: Jackfruit

Maavadu: Baby mangoes pickled in brine

Bakshanam: A collective name for deep-fried snacks (savoury and sweet)

Kutties: Little ones

Rava kesari: A sweet made of cream of wheat, clarified butter and sugar, garnished with fried cashews and raisins

Akka: Older sister

Rakshashi: Demoness

Kaapi: Decoction made from pouring steaming water over coffee grounds. Specific to South India

Murukku: Deep-fried rice snack known for its distinctive swirls that come from handcrafting it.

Lemon rice: Rice mixed with the juice of lemons and garnished with a tempering of mustard seeds, curry leaves and green chillies.

Maami: A generic term for middle-aged women in South India.

Dosai: Thin, savoury crepes made from fermented rice-lentil batter.

Chutney: A spicy dip typically made from coconut, green chilles and salt.

Pattama: A term of endearment that approximates to 'my silken one'.

CSK: Abbreviation for Chennai Super Kings, a cricket team in the International Premier League.

Poori: A deep-fried bread made from wheat flour.

Aloo Masala: Side of mashed potatoes with onions, tomatoes and green chillies.

Kannu: A term of endearment

Naada: Drawstring that is used with the salwar.

Peon: Admin staff who runs errands in offices.

Chellam: A term of endearment that means 'dear'

Ammu: A term of endearment

Paapa: Tamil word for baby

Thambi: Younger brother

Ayyo: A term of annoyance or surprise.

Kannamma: A term of endearment.

Ulla Vaango: Ulla Vaango is to ask someone to come inside respectfully.

Maapilai: A term for son-in-law in Tamil.

Printed in Great Britain
by Amazon